YELL
Erasures from *The Yellow Wallpaper*

Sarah Sousa

C&R Press
Conscious & Responsible

Summer Tide Pool Chapbook
2018 6th Collection Selection 1 of 1 CB 11

All Rights Reserved

Printed in the United States of America

First Edition
1 2 3 4 5 6 7 8 9

This book is a work of fiction. Any references to historical events, real people, or real places are used fictitiously. Other names, characters, places, and events are products of the author's imagination, and any resemblance to actual events or places or persons, living or dead, is entirely coincidental.

Selections of up to two pages may be reproduced without permissions. To reproduce more than two pages of any one portion of this book write to C&R Press publishers John Gosslee & Andrew Sullivan

Cover art and design by Max Rippon
Interior by Rachel Krumenacker

Copyright © 2019 Sarah Sousa

ISBN:978-1-949540-07-9

C&R Press
Conscious & Responsible
crpress.org

For special discounted bulk purchases, please contact sales@crpress.org
To book events, readings, and author signings please contact info@crpress.org

YELL

Table of Contents

I was more entertainment	1
There is one place	2
This damp want	3
Dear	4
We thought and lay there	5
I am alone a good deal	6
He said two beds	7
My enthusiastic keeper	8
Nothing living	9
Relief to my not-get-well	10
I felt I was a draught	11
I am serious night	12
Looked at one way	13
I think straight	14
It is so hard to talk	15
Have I after all	16
I know you	17
You are well underway	18
That a step	19
I didn't realize for a long time	20
How reason 'vokes	21
She said I stain everything	22
Believe by the moonlight	23
I have found out	24
I can only see one	25
She had a good deal	26
Her, merrily roped-up	27
Said he	28

I was more entertainment
than a toy-store.
        The knobs
of the big bureau
            winked.

     Remember,
                we ravaged
the chair, gouged
            the floor. You were
closer than a brother,
            I,
all the fierce sisters
we found in this bed.

There is one place,
the *right* spot
(a little higher)
and you'll find me
stimulating
as fireworks, up
        and down,
and sideways.
Positively everlasting.
I must not think about that.
I'll lie awake
and get too animate

This damp want
      disturbs
the parlor,
the stairs.
Such fast and trying.
I think this hard
all the time.
It used to climb me,
burning. That rough
gotten-off. I,
one in every woman,
me, most women,
shake before morning.

Dear,
I know our appetite.
It weigh a bit.
Her little heart
it be as sick
as the last hour.
"You won't go away?"
How can I, dear?
"Did in body perhaps."
Darling. I never for one instant.
There is nothing so like yours.
You not trust me any?

'Course, I said
"no."

We thought and lay there
        together.
Same light. Candle-law
is enough and unenough.
      The pang?
I mastered it but just.

I am alone a good deal
in my mind: riotous
             people
give way to whim,
gnarled fancy.
      In the cellar,
a horrid goose
with white running out.
Mystery flowers in beds.

Then he took me
in his rental arms,
my renovated dear,
and excited all
manner of needs.

He said two beds.
He said so pretty,
old-fashioned.
      I was perfect
    rest.
You depend, said he,
on air,
but air is big,
absorbed galore.
With little rings
and things, air
is a gymnasium
of air

My enthusiastic keeper
commands
certain light, velvet
meadows, the sun
faded just so. He sees
to
        everything now.

Nothing living.
Not soul
or ordinary matter.
A haunt?
Fate untenanted?
Or, the worst thing,
mere phosphates, phosphites,
but with a mind
to think about my condition.

Relief to my not-get-well.
It is, he says, the uses.
Tonics and trouble.
I disagree.
The years still and change.
What else is one to do?
Write for a while?
Meet with heavy want?
Be sensitive
        and more.
Be worse,
be bad.

I felt I was a draught
and couldn't shut
the window.

I am afraid
of moonlight.

I take pains
to make self.

There is some-
thing strange
about me.

I am serious night,
patterns and angles
slow to destroy
        themselves,
faded yet
in some places, lurid.
A smoldering sulfur
yell, unheard.

Looked at one way
I can almost fancy
I have hands.
 They connect
like a horizontal confusion:
Romanesque, grotesque,
laws of sprawling
 symmetry.
They rush off like the sea
chasing delirium.

I think straight.
I have
reasoning, want
to, feel able
to, love,
       hate. I know it's
absurd, but in his arms
and on the bed
he said I was rare
meat, his darling
and comfort and all.

It is so hard to talk.
I tried it last night,
it was slow
as moonlight.
She wants to get out.
Dear hate, darling danger.
I could shake the pattern.
Faint figure go walking.

Have I after all
just to wish-mention it?
Keep watch on that paper,
a strip of my head
nailed halfway round
the room, good
@pattern. Its shape
straight and stoop,
one and I.
The I-felt-behind
wanted I went.
I came.

I know you
are gaining flesh
and would go away
in an instant.
I feel sick about you.
There is nothing
so dangerous as a body.

You are well underway:
mind, face, front, back.
You are budding
while I sleep
like paper
and that is that.
Change slaps you,
shoots through, knocks
down, tramples you.
It is like a bad dream that I like.

That a step
might be
so fast.
I am hidden.
I don't want
to go outside.
For me,
outside is green
instead of yellow.
But my wall
is no use now
he's a door.

I didn't realize for a long time
what the thing was,
now I'm sure
it is a woman I was.
I watch it by night:
moonlight, candlelight, lamplight.
There is a woman

behind my quiet.
He started
the habit of making me
lie, subdued. I mean,
I sleep all I can.
But you see,
I'm convinced I don't sleep.
I'm getting a little afraid
I'm awake.

How reason 'vokes.
Curse my duty.
    Here I am
able to dress it.
    Hate never was
about this wall,
but what I let give-way.

She said I stain everything
that touches me.

Did that sound innocent?

I have watched her
when she did not know I was
looking, a scientific looking.
I've caught her eating my paper,
yellow smooches on her hands.

Sometimes
I see shadows
on her,
lying in wait.

I strike her,
in a quiet,
        quiet voice.
More spite
than restrain.

Believe by the moonlight
there is a moon.
At night light becomes
bars, woman behind.
I wake up and surprise it
lying in my bed,
straight and long,
the color of night.
I wonder how
it was done
and who did it.

I have found out
there are many women—
bright spots, shady spots,
so many heads, white
eyes. The pattern tries
to strangle them.
      They shake
the windows, the garden
and arbors.
      They shake
the daylight
    hard.

I can only see one
at a time: She
On the Long Road,
She Under Vines, Little Her,
The Night Woman,
Cloud Shadow,
The One I Do Not Trust,
Myself.

She had a good deal
of sleep to give.
I slept in the daytime
and at night. For months
she was sleeping
under the paper.
I wanted to sleep
professionally.
She looked sleep in the eyes,
loving and kind.
      Sly thing!
She shook.
I pulled.
We peeled sleep bare.

Her, merrily roped-up.
Vicious woman-doe.
Get back
behind herself.
But I could-am-will not
move. She tried.
I bit off my teeth,
clean off. That great,
angry end.
Now she is gone
and she is gone.

You can't open it.

Pound.
I shall axe
or break down or

Said he:
darling.
Said I:
"the key."
Of course
"the door."
That man
      my path

every time

C&R PRESS CHAPBOOKS

C&R Press hosts two chapbook selection periods from June to September and November to March coupled with a reading in New York City each year. The Winter Soup Bowl and Summer Tide Pool Chapbook Series are open to new and established writers in poetry, fiction, essay and other creative writing.

2018 Winter Soup Bowl
Yell by Sarah Sousa

2018 Winter Soup Bowl
Paleotemptestology by Bertha Crombet
White Boys from Hell by Jeffrey Skinner

2017 Summer Tide Pool
Atypical Cells of Undetermined Significance by Brenna Womer

2017 Winter Soup Bowl
Heredity and Other Inventions by Sharona Muir
On Inaccuracy by Joe Manning

2016 Summer Tide Pool
Cuntstruck by Kate Northrop
Relief Map by Erin M. Bertram
Love Undefined by Jonathan Katz

2016 Winter Soup Bowl
Notes from the Negro Side of the Moon by Earl Braggs
A Hunger Called Music: A Verse History in Black Music by Meredith Nnoka

C&R PRESS TITLES

NONFICTION

Women in the Literary Landscape by Doris Weatherford, et al
Credo: An Anthology of Manifestos & Sourcebook for Creative Writing by Rita Banerjee and Diana Norma Szokolyai

FICTION

Last Tower to Heaven by Jacob Paul
No Good, Very Bad Asian by Lelund Cheuk
Surrendering Appomattox by Jacob M. Appel
Made by Mary by Laura Catherine Brown
Ivy vs. Dogg by Brian Leung
While You Were Gone by Sybil Baker
Cloud Diary by Steve Mitchell
Spectrum by Martin Ott
That Man in Our Lives by Xu Xi

SHORT FICTION

Notes From the Mother Tongue by An Tran
The Protester Has Been Released by Janet Sarbanes

ESSAY AND CREATIVE NONFICTION

In the Room of Persistent Sorry by Kristina Marie Darling
the internet is for real by Chris Campanioni
Immigration Essays by Sybil Baker
Je suis l'autre: Essays and Interrogations by Kristina Marie Darling
Death of Art by Chris Campanioni

POETRY

A Family is a House by Dustin Pearson
The Miracles by Amy Lemmon
Banjo's Inside Coyote by Kelli Allen
Objects in Motion by Jonathan Katz
My Stunt Double by Travis Denton
Lessons in Camoflauge by Martin Ott
Millenial Roost by Dustin Pearson
Dark Horse by Kristina Marie Darling
All My Heroes are Broke by Ariel Francisco
Holdfast by Christian Anton Gerard
Ex Domestica by E.G. Cunningham
Like Lesser Gods by Bruce McEver
Notes from the Negro Side of the Moon by Earl Braggs
Imagine Not Drowning by Kelli Allen
Notes to the Beloved by Michelle Bitting
Free Boat: Collected Lies and Love Poems by John Reed
Les Fauves by Barbara Crooker
Tall as You are Tall Between Them by Annie Christain

www.ingramcontent.com/pod-product-compliance
Lightning Source LLC
Chambersburg PA
CBHW032106040426
42449CB00007B/1203